ECO FRIENDLY PROMOTIONAL PRODUCT GUIDE

A Green Marketing Handbook
for Small Business

Heidi Thorne

CONTENTS

GREEN VS. GREEN

Does anyone really care about green marketing these days?

Remember when it seemed like everyone was trying to "go green?" I do. And since that whole going green thing aligns with many of my personal values, I became an expert of sorts on eco friendly promotions around 2008 or so. Offering green products seemed to align so well with the zeitgeist, and almost none of my direct or near competitors were even focusing on green. I thought this would give me a clear competitive edge.

Ramped up a blog on eco friendly promotions. Focused my main shop site on eco friendly products. Talked with customers and networking connections about it. And then, drum roll please... nothing.

I got a few customers who wanted to show their greenness with reusable bags or recycled pens. But the results were dismal at best.

Then a different kind of "green" issue reared its ugly head: recession. I had one client bluntly tell me that if there was a five or ten cent difference between a standard product and an eco friendly version, she would go with the standard product every time. Love good honest feedback.

So was green marketing a fad that fizzled? Yes and no. Yes, the "we're green" horn tooting seems to have died down quite a bit due to the economy. But, no, greener products, procedures and policies are here to stay.

I've written this book primarily for marketers who are in small to mid-size organizations and are looking for green marketing ideas that don't take much of the other green (you know, the one with a "$" before it).

At its core, going green is really a habit, not just an event, project or product choice. With repeated practice and commitment it becomes automatic. All the buying and implementation principles in this book are simple so that the habit can be achieved with as little cost and effort as possible.

Through small steps like these, we can all help to make this world a greener place.

CHAPTER 1:
ECO FRIENDLY
DEFINITIONS

Before we get too far discussing green promotional product issues, let's review the key terms you'll need to know to make educated buying decisions.

All definitions are arranged in alphabetical order and do not suggest ranking or priority.

Biodegradable. Product containing material that will naturally dissolve or disintegrate when exposed to weather elements or when placed in landfill/composting conditions. Usually this term refers to materials that either do this naturally or are enhanced to degrade within a short period of time (could be less than 5 or 10 years in some cases). Biodegradable products are typically made from plant or animal matter (see also degradable). Helps eliminate build up of waste material in landfills.

Carbon Footprint. Measurement of the level of carbon produced by the manufacture, distribution, use, and disposal of a product. Carbon levels can also be measured for events and personal lifestyle. See also *offsets*.

Degradable. Product that will disintegrate when exposed to elements (rain, sunlight, etc.) or when deposited into landfills. While all materials are degradable given time (hundreds or thousands or years for some plastics), usually this term refers to materials that either do this naturally or are enhanced to degrade within a short period of time (could be less than 5 or 10 years in some cases). Degradable plastics may be made of petroleum products enhanced with additives to shorten degradation time or to degrade into more earth-friendly substances (see also *biodegradable*). Helps eliminate build up of waste material in landfills.

Eco Friendly. Term loosely used to describe any product, process, or person that helps save energy, eliminate waste, or prevent harm to people or the planet.

Fair Trade. A method of doing business that seeks to: pay fair prices/wages and benefits for products and services; provide safe and healthy working and living conditions; insists on accountability; and, promotes environmental responsibility. This is of particular concern in developing nations which have suffered exploitation. Fair trade policies prohibit the use of child, forced, or prison labor in the manufacture of goods.

Natural. Material or product derived from a plant or animal source. May or may not be organic. See *organic* definition below.

Offsets. A donation made by a company to balance any environmentally damaging effects of their manufacturing, business activities, or event, particularly carbon emissions. For example, a manufacturer may purchase credits for their excessive carbon footprint which would go towards environmentally supportive efforts such as wind or solar energy projects. To calculate your carbon footprint or to make an offset donation, visit www.carbonfund.org.

Organic. Material or product derived from a plant or

animal source using organic methods. Organic methods do not use chemical herbicides, pesticides, or genetically modified organisms (GMO). They may use energy and water saving equipment and processes. Organic materials cannot be processed using the same facilities and equipment used for non-organic methods. To be labeled as organic, material or product must be verified by a third party such as the USDA (U.S. Dept. of Agriculture). Organic materials cannot be processed using the same facilities and equipment used for non-organic methods.

Pre-Consumer. Waste material resulting from manufacturing processes that has not yet been used or consumed by an end user.

Post-Consumer. Waste material that has been used at least once by an end user.

Recyclable. Product or material that can be melted, shredded, disassembled, or otherwise broken down and remanufactured for use in another product. These can include glass, plastic, fabric, wood, metals, and paper. Plastics are usually rated with a recycling symbol to indicate chemical composition and/or recyclability. Helps divert volume of waste going into landfills.

Recycled. Product or material made from a waste product. Content can include pre-consumer or post-consumer content or both.

Renewable. Can describe a product, material, or energy source that can be easily replenished, with low or no environmental damage or cost, when depleted.

Reusable. Any product that can be used more than once. The more times it can be used, the longer it takes to make its way to a landfill. May also be made of recyclable material which can further divert materials from landfills.

Socially Responsible. A broad term to describe the labor

policies used in the manufacture of a product or material. Can also refer to a manufacturer's commitment to community development or charitable efforts.

Sustainable. Synonymous with renewable. Usually refers to products, materials, or energy sources that are easily replenished, with low or no environmental damage or cost, when depleted.

Third Party Verification. Government and non-government organizations can provide certification that a specific methodology or policy was adhered to during the manufacture of a specific product. Labor policies and organic farming methods are two areas that can be verified. One such certifying organization is Oregon Tilth for organic products and the U.S. Department of Agriculture (USDA).

CHAPTER 2: ECO FRIENDLY PROMOTIONAL PRODUCT SHOPPING GUIDELINES (OR BUY THIS, NOT THAT)

Is there some sort of ranking of eco friendly-ness? Yes. When shopping for promotional products that are better for our planet, here are, in order, the factors to consider:

Recycled (with Post-Consumer Content). These products truly help close the green loop by keeping waste products out of landfills and reducing the amount of virgin material being created from resources that are not easily renewable such as petroleum.

Recycled (with Pre-Consumer Content). Well, at least

these products keep the waste from manufacturing out of landfills. Has been going on for a long time as a standard manufacturing process to reduce waste and costs. So the product you're buying may already have been a "recycled" product. Now manufacturers are just telling you about it.

Biodegradable. In theory, everything is biodegradable; it just depends on how many years it takes and what it biodegrades into. If a product is labeled as "biodegradable," it typically is made from a substance that will break down, dissolve or disintegrate within a short period of time when compared to standard plastics which could survive for millennia. Some will degrade if exposed to elements or landfill conditions in as less than a decade. Also, biodegradable products are usually formulated to degrade into either non-harming or even beneficial residues. See specific product info for details since not all biodegradable products are made from the same material or biodegrade in the same way. Only issue with biodegradable is that it does require the continuous manufacture of new material, even if it is eco friendly or sustainable.

Recyclable. These products may or may not include recycled content, but can be thrown into the recycling stream (where facilities exist) and be resurrected into other products, again, closing the green loop.

Reusable. One of the weakest of the eco friendly claims, but does carry some weight if the product typically is a throwaway that now can be used again. If purchasing a reusable promotional product, one that is also recyclable when its reusing days are over is the most earth-friendly choice.

Buying Local. With less fuel needed to transport your purchase to you, you help conserve oil resources. However, in the promotional products arena, your distributor may live next door to you, but the product you purchase from them may be coming from across the country. Plus, inputs to the manufacture of the product can be from anywhere in the world. A difficult to qualify eco friendly claim.

Socially Responsible. Uses unionized, local/home country, or fair trade labor. Also may tout charitable donations made with each purchase. Not so much an eco friendly choice (except if a donation is made to an environmental cause) as a feel good or community driven choice.

Want to know how your promotional products rate? See the Green Promo Score Sheet in Chapter 8.

CHAPTER 3: BIODEGRADABLE PROMOTIONAL PRODUCTS - ARE THEY REALLY?

Every other week or so I'll see an article or a blog post about how biodegradable products cannot be called biodegradable because of the nature of the landfills in which they are deposited. The point is well taken. So before we start talking about biodegradable promotional products, let's discuss some known facts so that we stay on topic (and so that I don't get a flood of didn't-you-know comments afterwards).

Agreed, many landfills are reported to be poorly managed, meaning that they lack key ingredients such as sufficient oxygen, water, sunlight, and microbes which can aid in the biodegrading process. Landfills are also often packed tightly which also inhibits the process.

As well, there are limited composting waste facilities. These are primarily dedicated to yard waste and food scrap. I suppose some biodegradable promotional products could find their way there, although that scenario is not customary.

Lastly, I am not discussing ALL biodegradable products or packaging in this article. The focus is on "promotional products" which include imprinted plastic pens, mugs, desk items, and the like which are sold through distributors to businesses, schools, and organizations to help promote themselves and events.

As of this writing, a large number of biodegradable products in our niche market are made of corn. Corn plastic is biodegradable in composting conditions. But will it go there when disposed of? More likely it will go to a standard landfill. Will it degrade there as well? It would depend on the landfill conditions.

Other biodegradable materials used in these products are a mixture of plant-based plastics and may include petroleum-based material. Some are treated with additives to enhance their safe biodegradability under specific conditions. Will they properly degrade? Again, it depends on the landfill conditions and the particular material in question.

Hate to say "it depends." Whether a product will or will not degrade does depend on the landfill in which it is deposited. The fact is that they are made to break down under the conditions for which the material was designed. So, yes, they are technically biodegradable, but may not practically be so.

There is no doubt that labeling standards for disposal must be developed for biodegradable promotional products that are easily understood by consumers who buy or receive them. In this way, these items have a better chance of entering a waste or recycling stream where they will have less impact on the environment.

Until then, your choice comes down to this: 1) A bio-degradable product that has a chance, even if it is a small chance, of safely degrading after its useful life; or, 2) A standard petroleum-based plastic item that may not have a prayer of degrading until at least the next millennium. I think the choice is obvious.

CHAPTER 4:
DO FAIR TRADE PROMOTIONAL PRODUCTS EXIST?

Where was it made? Who made it? How was it made? What's in it? These are going to become very important questions as the concern over fair trade issues continues to grow, especially as the more socially conscious Generation Y demographic begins to have greater influence in the marketplace. To clarify, fair trade policies prohibit the use of child, forced or prison labor in the manufacture of goods, seek to pay fair wages, and emphasize accountability and environmental sustainability. This is a critical issue in much of the developing world.

In the area of promotional products (imprinted pens, mugs, T-shirts, etc.), fair trade choices are limited and often not clearly identified. This is not to say that those products that do not come with fair trade in their description don't qualify. In fact, many of them do. However, at present, it needs to be confirmed on a case by case basis and cannot be assumed. Fair trade certifications are available, but promotional products do not clearly fall under one

specific program, making it confusing for both distributors and their customers.

One way for marketers to ensure they are buying fair
trade promotional products is to limit choices to those
made in countries with established fair labor standards
such as the United States. That opens up some more options, but still quite limited. In a review of the Advertising Speciality Institute ESP Online database, about 10% of
products in major promotional product categories such as
pens, mugs, and T-shirts are USA made. There is also the
chance that some of the materials or components used in
manufacture were sourced from outside the United States;
however, to be classified as "made in the USA," the im-
ported materials or parts cannot be a significant portion of
the whole.

What should a marketer do to make more socially conscious choices?

Ask! Discuss your fair trade purchasing objectives with
your promotional product distributor or marketing con-
sultant. Ask for verification and/or certification that can
confirm the origin or compliance of the product.

Specify Made in the USA or Fair Trade Nation. If unsure
that your product choice qualifies, select an alternative
that is made in the United States or other fair trade nation.
The United States has well-established fair labor laws and
enforcement in place.

CHAPTER 5: PREPARING PROMOTIONS FOR THE AFTERLIFE

One of the challenges with eco friendly promotions is the issue of disassembly. Even if your product contains a lot of recycled materials, if it's really difficult to deconstruct it after its life is over, and it just has to go directly to the landfill, you really haven't gained too much.

Let's look at an example. Let's look at a standard imprinted 3-ring binder. When I purchased it, it had a sticker on it that said that it contained 100% recycled chip board. That's great. But if I wanted to get recycle this binder after I was done with it, I would have to cut apart the plastic to get to the chip board and to also release the plastic for recycling. As well, I would have to take apart the ring hardware here, so that the metal could be recycled. That's a lot of work, and a lot of people won't take those extra steps to make something recyclable.

Now let's look at an item that would be a greener choice in terms of the disassembly issue: A standard promotional stadium cup that's made of recycled and biodegradable plastic. If it's used at a sporting event, when people are done with it, they can just throw it in the regular trash because it is biodegradable as well. It's all molded of one piece, so you don't have to worry about any disassembly whatsoever.

So when you are thinking about green promotions, think about the next life after you're done with the initial promotion.

CHAPTER 6:
4 GREENER PROMOTIONAL PRODUCT DECORATING OPTIONS

You've selected an eco friendly promotional product that's recycled, biodegradable, recyclable, or at least reusable. But doesn't the imprinting process use petroleum-based inks which are bad for the environment? Yes, that may be true. So to make your choice greener all the way around, inquire whether any of these greener decorating options might be available:

1. Laser Etching. This inkless laser process etches your logo into the surface of a product. Basically the top layer of the surface is etched away, leaving the base surface to show through in the shape of your logo. Depending of the top and base surface colors, this may leave a very visible or a very subtle imprint. For example, if the top surface is a blue painted coating and the base surface is a silvery metallic, it will leave a silvery and very visible logo. However, if the surface is an unpainted metal, it may leave a logo that is substantially the same color as the product, but with a slightly different texture. Laser etching is generally done on metals and glass. Produces a sophisticated look with high imprint durability.

2. *Debossing.* Another inkless option, debossing uses heat to impress your logo into the surface of an item. Like laser etching, this will leave a subtle and sophisticated tone-on-tone look. Generally debossing is available on thicker surfaces that would respond to heat. Padded writing portfolios would be a prime example. It is also being used on recycled cardboard and leather surfaces. Offers high imprint durability.

3. *Embroidery.* While some of the dyes used in embroidery threads may or may not be totally green or organic, it is another option that does not employ application of petroleum-based inks.

4. *Water-Based Inks.* Particularly for promotional T-shirts, water-based inks are now available. This has not yet gained a foothold for other types of products.

CHAPTER 7: IS YOUR PROMOTIONAL T-SHIRT MADE OF UNNATURAL COTTON?

So I go to a "green" event and they hand out cotton canvas bags. The bags are reusable, sturdy and made from a non-petroleum product and that's good. However, conventionally grown cotton is one of the most non-eco friendly materials available for promotional T-shirts and bags.

One of my promotional wearables suppliers reported that traditionally grown cotton uses 25% of insecticides and 10% of the pesticides used in the entire world! They estimate that it takes 150 grams of pesticides and fertilizers to make one T-shirt. Chemical fungicides, herbicides, and defoliants are also used. Even to begin with, the cotton seeds are frequently GMOs (genetically modified organisms). Natural? Hardly.

Why is this? If cotton crops are not rotated, which can be the case in traditional cotton farming, soil becomes sterile and devoid of nutrients to foster healthy crops and fend off pests and diseases. Thus the need for genetically engineered seeds which are stronger, coupled with a healthy (??) dose of chemical support. Intensive irrigation is also required, sometimes up to tons (literally) of water.

And all of this doesn't even take into consideration the land use devoted to traditional cotton farming.

Contrast conventional cotton farming with a truly natural alternative: organic cotton. Organic cotton farming starts out with untreated non-GMO cotton seeds. The seeds are planted in fields where cotton crops are rotated to increase organic matter, build fertile soil, and increase water retention capability, thus reducing water needs. Natural pest predators, trap crops, and cultivation methods are used to eliminate pesticide use. Hand weeding methods as opposed to chemicals. Those of you who are gardeners know this is quite a job!

All equipment and processing of organic cotton must be done separately from traditional cotton to avoid contamination. Organic cotton must also be certified (look for it on product information or labeling) to ensure that each bale of cotton has been grown using organic methods and that it has remained uncontaminated throughout its journey from field to factory to buyer. With all the meticulous farming, processing, and monitoring required for organic cotton, it is often more expensive than conventional cotton.

While the manufacture of organic cotton is more earth and people friendly than traditional cotton, the fact remains that land use needed to produce cotton is significant. And though land use may still be an issue, we are also seeing entries in the promotional wearable and bag market that are made from soy, bamboo, corn, and other non-cotton plant-based sources.

Would you believe it if I told you that in some cases polyester fabrics are a more eco friendly choice? Granted, polyester is not typically degradable, though it can be recyclable. And most people prefer the comfort of cotton. But here's something to consider. A petrochemical plant used to create polyester and synthetic fibers might use just a fraction of the land mass that cotton does. A worthwhile tradeoff?

My prediction? Additives to enhance plastic degradability are becoming more common in promotional product offerings such as mugs. I think we might see manmade fabric T-shirts with enhanced degradability, too. Recycled polyester fibers are also creeping into the promotional product marketplace and help close the green loop by remanufacturing and repurposing fibers for new uses to keep them out of landfills.

CHAPTER 8: GREEN-O-METER

Okay, so you've decided to go greener with your promotional products buying. Great! Now, how do you figure what what's the greenest choice? Are there degrees of green-ness?

Yes, some products are eco friendly than others. But sometimes it's difficult to evaluate one against another. So that why we developed the Green Promo Score Sheet A screenshot of the tool is shown in the following figure.

Bet you didn't realize there were that many aspects of green promo buying, did you?

GREEN PROMO SCORE SHEET

Enter 1 for Yes, 0 for No, for Each Product Considered.

	Product #1	Product #2	Product #3
Recyclable?			
Reusable?			
Contains Any Recycled Content?			
Recycled Content Over 30% Post-Consumer?			
Organic?			
Made from Sustainable Resources (e.g., Bamboo)?			
Biodegradable?			
Water-Based, Soy-Based, Inkless (e.g., Laser Engraving) or Ink-Saving Imprint Processes Used?			
Factory Uses Renewable Energy or Follows Energy Saving Practices?			
Manufactured Locally/Regionally to Save Fuel for Shipping and Support Local Businesses?			
Made in USA which Supports Fair Labor Practices?			
Factory Uses Union Labor or Fair Labor Practices in Manufacturing Product?			
Factory Uses Union Labor or Fair Labor Practices for Imprinting?			
Manufacturer Publicly Supports Charity, Environmental Conservation, or Community Efforts?			
TOTALS			

© Copyright 2009 Heidi Thorne

CHAPTER 9: "I'LL BE GREEN TOMORROW" (BUT HERE'S WHAT YOU CAN DO TODAY)

Small to mid-size businesses are deferring "green" initiatives (along with many advertising expenditures I might add). Why? Because at this juncture it takes some green to go green. And if a company is bleeding red ink, the response is often *"I'll be green tomorrow."*

Much as I resist admitting it, green products are, in many cases, more expensive than their non-green counterparts. People ask if a product is made from recycled materials shouldn't it be cheaper? Not really, because reclaiming, recycling, repurposing, and reforming require new equipment and processes. We are definitely in the investment phase of the green movement. So expect prices on green products to remain higher for a while.

What can you do to begin instituting green initiatives in your promotions while still conserving funds?

Buy Less. As a distributor of promotional products, you

can imagine I'm not thrilled about saying this. But buying just what you need for a particular purpose or event will conserve funds and help eliminate waste (you know, the pens you bought three years ago that are dried out but still sitting on your storage shelves and will eventually have to be thrown away).

Buy More. Okay, I like this one better. Even though it sounds contradictory to the preceding point, buying in bulk saves funds and the environment in multiple ways. First, you save by gaining volume price discounts. Second, packaging in bulk for shipping eliminates extra boxes for multiple small orders. Third, it comes to you in one trip, saving fuel and shipping charges that would be incurred over multiple orders. But always analyze your usage rate and calculate your need for the next ONE YEAR period. Many promotional products, particularly pens, do have a shelf and usable life. My rule of thumb for pens and paper products shelf life is maximum one to two years. My rule of thumb for the time it will take for you to get bored with your own promotions is six months to one year. So plan for shelf life and your need for novelty.

One Step at a Time. It can feel so overwhelming at first. So just take it one step at a time. When you run out of one of your usual promotional products, restock it with a greener product. Notice I didn't necessarily say "green" product. If you've been using traditional petroleum-based products, restock with one that contains a bit of recycled content, choosing a greener product each time you re-order. Also notice that I said when you run out. Don't toss out cash in the trash by discarding your non-green items just so you can feel good about going green. Use 'em up before they head out for recycling or waste.

Buy Local. Promotional products are made and distributed from many points throughout the United States. Here at Thorne Communications we always look for suppliers that are as close as possible to our clients to save time, shipping costs, and fuel. We work with several that are right here in the Midwest to serve our strong Chicago area client base.

Use Double Duty Promotions. Especially around the holidays, select gifts that pack a 2-for-1 punch, such as a food gift packaged in a reusable container. Not only will you be giving two gifts which are always appreciated, you'll be giving a promotion that will keep your brand in front of your customers long after the first gift is gone.

CHAPTER 10: WHEN ECO FRIENDLY PROMOTIONAL PRODUCTS DON'T WORK

With our society's emphasis on green issues, it might seem unthinkable that there would be occasions not to use eco friendly promotional products. But there are.

Let's look at one in particular. An office equipment dealer received most of his promotional products from a manufacturer he represented. One of the products was reusable grocery totes. Nice gesture. But did it support his efforts of selling office equipment? No. Hope these bags aren't residing in a landfill somewhere.

What are the occasions when an eco friendly choice is not appropriate?

When It Doesn't Align With Your Product or Service. It seems that everyone is giving our reusable tote and grocery bags these days. Let's say you develop software for manufacturing, Does it make sense to have your customers flaunting your name and website in the local grocery store? Probably not. You've just wasted an important "green" resource: your money. That being said, when you do find a product that is appropriate for your business, seeking a greener version of it is the right thing to do.

When Your Company Has Not Made a Commitment to Green Initiatives. Integrity alert! Using eco friendly promotional products when your company has not yet made a commitment to going greener sends mixed signals to your customers and prospects, decreasing your trust factor.

When You Don't Really Need to Buy Anything. A key earth-friendly principle is to reduce your consumption. If you do have less environmentally friendly promotional products in your supply room, don't run out to buy a greener product just to feel good. Use up what you have and then restock with a greener alternative when you run out.

CHAPTER 11:
WHEN TO BUY AND WHEN TO BYPASS REUSABLE BAGS

We all know that using reusable bags for shopping, events or trade shows are a great idea for the environment because it reduces or eliminates the need for single-use plastic bags. But we're fast approaching a time when their green value may have peaked.

We're getting to a point where we're going to have reusable bag glut, where people are going to get so many of them, they're just going to stuff them away somewhere, or worst case scenario, they're going to throw them out into the trash. That's really bad because then we've created more garbage than what we had originally intended.

I think the best strategy for going forward with bags is to really evaluate whether you need to provide a bag for your event attendees or your customers. It will be a green thing for you to do, and it will also save you some green as well.

So how do you know if you should buy or bypass providing reusable promotional bags for your event or customers? Ask yourself these questions:

1. Will conference attendees or customers naturally be bringing their own bags, briefcases and backpacks? Bypass. Important Note: If you do decide to ditch the distribution of reusable promotional bags at an event, alert attendees in advance so they know to bring their own.

2. Do you have a lot of small items that need to be distributed to attendees? Buy. It will speed the distribution process at registration and eliminate the need for multiple small bags.

3. Does the bag design allow for use in multiple scenarios, i.e. shopping, conferences, work? Buy. Look for those with longer handles that allow over-the-shoulder or hand carry use. Also look for those with sturdy fabrics for longer wear.

CHAPTER 12: HOW TO GREEN UP PROMOTIONAL T-SHIRT BUYING WITH LIFE CYCLE ASSESSMENT

Have you ever thought about what happens to your imprinted T-shirt after your event? It's a good question and one that you really need to think about BEFORE buying.

Ideally, of course, you'd like to think that your T-shirt will be worn by recipients as they work out, shop at the store, or go to other events. Unfortunately, that's not the case.

Here are some of the more popular post-event lives for imprinted T-shirts:

Pajamas. Yes, they will have lots of market exposure while people sleep. Not!

Car Wash Rags. Especially if they're white and don't have a lot of printing on them.

Gardening/Housework Attire. It's not appropriate enough to wear out on the street. So it's okay to mess it up while doing dirty work.

Charity/Resale Donation. Your T-shirt could be going straight to the donation bin after your event.

Let's take a moment to talk about charity donations. It surprises many people to learn that charities don't always sell these castoffs in their resale stores. Items that are not considered suitable for sale on a resale level are often sold by weight to jobbers who sell them to a variety of markets both here and abroad.

Don't be disheartened by the fate of your event T-shirt going somewhere other than to a needy person in another country or being shredded for other use. In the promotional arena, there is a new market for recycled fiber fabrics. Both cottons and synthetic fibers are being repurposed into new T-shirts and fleece items.

Knowing the life cycle (and afterlife) of that promotional T-shirt project you're planning is key to making a greener purchase. Specifically, you need to assess:

Potential Lifetime. How long, in terms of months or years, would you expect recipients to wear it? Will they wear it at the event and send it directly to the charity bin? Some of this can be determined by the quality of the shirt you choose. Higher quality or very comfortable ones, regardless of imprint, can become favorites. I've received some at athletic events that I immediately sent to the donation pile. The fabrics were cheap, itchy, wrinkly, had an imprint that used so much ink I thought I was wearing a plastic bag, or, in the case of a "tech" fabric, so hot I sweat in them instantly. Goodbye! Also, to help extend the shirt's life post-donation, opt for limiting imprint areas to expand the useful fabric area. Imprinted areas are often unusable except for scrap fiber.

Your Recipients. Are your recipients T-shirt wearers? I've done a lot of running events and I've observed that a lot of the runners are very unlikely to wear the event shirt at the race. Very competitive runners or athletes do NOT typically wear them on race day. They wear their training gear or, what I call, "good luck wear." They may wear the event shirt after the event, but typically not for training. Really the only ones they want are those for high profile competitive running events such as marathons. It becomes a badge of honor they'll be proud to display! But for fun runs and community type events, maybe not so much (a box of free energy bars might be more appreciated). By contrast, at a fun run/walk, you may have a lot of families where a wearable freebie might help stretch the clothing budget for kids. Plus, kids might want to show off that they were cool enough to participate. So, yes, they want them.

Collectible Potential. How much do you think you could get on an online auction for a vintage rock concert T-shirt? Probably a good buck! Is the promotional shirt you're buying going to promote a once-in-a-lifetime experience? Does it commemorate an up-and-coming artist that could make it valuable in the future? This may be difficult to assess. Generally, though, the higher profile the event, performer, or place visited, the more collectible market value the shirt may have down the road.

Extended Promotional Value. Shirts which promote a continuing effort, such as awareness campaigns, may have an extended life after an initial event. In this case you would be well advised to select a wear-worthy choice that is comfortable and better quality to foster continued post-event wear.

Supply Chain. Sometimes this is tricky. Most promotional online vendors rarely, if ever, identify the country of origin for T-shirts. It can vary widely from product to product. As well, in the case of overseas production, source country could change rapidly should the manufacturer move operations to circumvent quota issues. I have seen T-shirt samples of the exact same shirt style that have different countries of origin on each. If fair trade issues are a concern, stick with USA-made T-shirts. Should you be more concerned about a greener fabric content—for example, you don't want cotton made with pesticides or herbicides —then stick with organics. To be labeled organic, it must be processed separately.

Whew! That was quite a journey. Bottom line? You need to think outside the event or promotion when purchasing.

CHAPTER 13: 3 EXIT STRATEGIES TO GREEN YOUR TRADE SHOW OR EVENT

Ah, the irony! While a presentation drones on about the evils of plastic water bottles and what should be done about it, attendees at a green new product showcase search for a place to pitch their now empty plastic water bottles. A showcase host replies, *"You know, we hadn't thought about that. Just throw them in the regular trash."*

In case you're wondering, yes, this really happened.

Making your tradeshow or event greener is a start-to-finish affair. What we'll be looking at here are "exit strategies" you can use to make sure your green efforts don't go walking out the door when your event ends.

1. Bins for Used Lanyards and Name Badges at Exit. Unless the lanyard is super-cool or your event is attended by those who need them for their security badges, it is unlikely that event attendees will ever use them again in the future. Same goes for the plastic badge holders. Why not collect them at the event exit and reuse them for next time? This will not only help the earth, but will save you money since you can buy less for the next event. (See the chapter on *Yuck! A Dark Side of Going Green at Events* for additional discussion and concerns on this topic.)

2. Bins for Plastic, Paper, and Aluminum Waste at Exit. The amount of these waste materials generated at events can be huge. With still low recycling rates at the individual level, chances are the pile of paper, plastic containers, and cans will promptly be pitched into the straight-to-landfill waste stream in a hurry once they leave the building. Tap in to people's desire to unload unnecessary weight at the end of an event and provide separated recycling bins at the exit. Unless you plan to haul it away yourself, this effort will have to be coordinated with the event facility for pick-up.

3. Recycle or Ship Back Show Materials. It's the last few hours of an event and what do you see? Booth personnel scrambling to get rid of show materials so they don't have to pack, ship or drag them back home. What a waste on multiple levels! If you are stuffing brochures or promotional products into the hands of unwilling show visitors, where do you think those items will end up? Of course, in the trash, likely as soon as they leave the show. These materials will also likely end up in the landfill-bound trash, not recycling bin. If you unnecessarily hand out show materials, you will probably have to reorder or reprint them for another event. So you have increased costs for the earth and your marketing budget. Plan in advance how you will handle the return or recycling of unused show materials and advise your booth personnel of procedures.

CHAPTER 14: YUCK! A DARK SIDE OF GOING GREEN AT EVENTS

I had quite a revelation about tradeshow and event lanyards at a conference. What I learned is that many people often enjoy getting them as souvenirs. So let's call them badges (pun intended) of honor. But for event veterans (like me), I don't need another lanyard for sure!

And for those in the events world who want to go greener for both the environment and their budgets, recycling lightly used lanyards at future events seems like a great idea.

But while at a conference, I was chatting some of my event industry pals about greener meetings. Mentioned the idea of collecting and recycling lanyards at future events. There was an *"eeewww"* response, although it sounded like a logical solution. Makeup, oils, personal products and more can accumulate on them making some give pause to using a recycled lanyard. Also, washing them is either not possible or practical. Truly a dark side to going green for this particular item at meetings.

Guess that scenario really never crossed my mind, probably because I'm not too much of a germaphobe (I have two big always-a-mess dogs). But I have to realize that there are others not so inclined.

So now what? Are we going to have to continue to buy new lanyards for every event, only to have them pitched into the garbage after maybe 10-20 hours of wear? Hmm... what to do?

Here are some thoughts...

Still Collect and Recycle, But Offer New. I'm going to guess that some people are like me and using a recycled lanyard doesn't faze them. What event and tradeshow planners can do is still collect the lanyards and offer a recycled one to attendees, but also have a stash of brand new ones for those who are more sensitive on this issue or those who collect them as souvenirs.

B.Y.O.B.L. No, not Bring Your Own Booze & Liquor (although some might). How about Bring Your Own Badge/Lanyard? No doubt, if you have a gathering of regular conference goers, they have quite a stockpile of these little-used gizmos. Many may also use them every day on the job. Give them a bit of a reward if they agree to bring and use their own badge and lanyard. Less cost for you and the planet.

CHAPTER 15:
HOW TO START
AN ECO FRIENDLY
CASUAL FRIDAY

By now, Casual Fridays are a standard business practice in many companies. But what if you could take that concept one step further and encourage eco friendly values by creating Eco Friendly Casual Fridays?

An Eco Friendly Casual Friday would still allow the business casual dress code of a standard Casual Friday. However, employees would be encouraged to wear at least one piece of eco friendly apparel. Eco friendly apparel options would include items that are made with organic, sustainable, biodegradable or recycled materials. You might also want to add social consciousness categories to this list such as fair trade, USA made, and union made.

Sounds easy enough. But once you start looking for the eco friendly (or fair trade) label in many popular clothing retailers, you'll find that items qualifying for one or more of these categories are scarce. What's more is that it is often impossible to determine if an item qualifies while shopping in the store. You would have to do some significant supply chain research to determine many items' qualifications.

With the retail arena scenario as it presently is, you might want to provide a way for employees to share why the item they chose to wear is eco friendly and where they purchased the item. That way they can assist fellow employees in finding good eco friendly sources and make it an educational exercise as well.

What would employees gain from this exercise? First, employees would become aware of how non-eco friendly many of their everyday purchases are. The goal would be to encourage them to vote with their wallets by redirecting spending to those items and retailers that are aligned with these values.

There may be some resistance by employees to participate because they may not share eco friendly values. So whatever you do, do not turn this into a battleground. Just make it a fun program to participate in. You might even want to start a contest to reward those who wear either the greatest number of eco friendly clothing items on a given day or those who wear the most eco friendly items (i.e. 100% organic, post-consumer recycled, etc.). A gift card to an eco friendly clothing retailer would be an appropriate prize.

To jumpstart the program, why not consider imprinting some eco friendly promotional T-shirts with your company name to distribute to your staff? That way those who may not be very interested in expending effort or money to find their own eco friendly clothing can at least participate by wearing the company-provided T-shirt.

If your business is already in the eco friendly arena or instituting green initiatives, establishing an Eco Friendly Casual Friday would be a way to help bolster these values in your company and, through your employees, to the community at large.

CHAPTER 16: EARTH DAY AND ARBOR DAY PROMOTIONAL PRODUCT YOU SHOULD NEVER USE

Right on the heels of Earth Day is Arbor Day on the last Friday in April. What seems like a natural promotional product to give away to celebrate these green holidays? Tree seedlings. What's the one promotional product you should NEVER buy to promote these celebrations? You guessed it, tree seedlings. Why? Isn't it good for the environment to have more trees?

Yes, it is good to have trees, lots of trees, in our communities. They help filter the air of pollutants, provide shade and cooling to buildings, and are just delightful to view.

However, what people forget when giving away tree seedlings is that the little sprout could one day reach a height of 40 feet or more, with a drip line (the spread of the tree's root system) that could be up to 12 feet diameter or more. So an improperly planted tree's root system could interfere with anything that is within that drip line circumference, including sewer and water systems, foundations, and other structures.

Trees require special care when planting to survive and thrive. If planted too close together, the trees will not have enough room to spread their growth and could fall into ill health or restrict the growth of other surrounding shrubs and trees. They also require some careful watering to establish themselves properly. Once a tree's health fails, it may need to be removed, sometimes at an expense into the hundreds or thousands of dollars.

Plus, neighboring properties could be impacted by either a tree's roots or growth. That is not a way to make friends in your neighborhood.

A better promotional product for these environmentally friendly holidays would be products are made of recycled paper. That will really help keep our planet filled with trees!

CHAPTER 17: WHY AREN'T THERE MORE GREEN CONSUMERS?

Why aren't more consumers recycling and buying more earth-friendly products? What's wrong with them? Actually, it's not what's wrong with them. It's what's missing from our communities and businesses.

Here are some examples that will illustrate the situation.

* I'm waiting in line at a local coffee house. A mother and her daughter are getting ready to leave and are searching for the recycle bins for their used beverage cups. The mother asks the counter person about it. The clearly Generation Y worker replies that they would like to offer bins to customers, but their waste hauling company will not pick up recycling waste.

* After years of only being provided a small bin for recyclable material, our local waste company has provided residents with large, wheeled containers for it. Score one for the waste company! However, the instructions on the container are very vague about what can and cannot be

placed in it. What recycling codes are accepted? What types of paper can be included? So we just throw everything that even seems recyclable in it. Is it being more finely sorted at the recycling site? One has to wonder.

* What should one do with hazardous household waste such as cleaning chemicals, prescription medications, paint, etc.? The proper thing to do is bring it to an official drop-off site for disposal. In my area, which is a suburb of a large city, the year-round drop-off site is about 15 miles away. That will take about 20-30 minutes of drive time each way minimum. Plus, it will use one to two gallons of gasoline. Gain one for the environment, lose one for the environment.

* Then there's the build-up of e-waste. Many communities in our area are holding recycling days where residents can drop off old monitors, computers, printers, etc. This is an excellent idea. At the last event in our area, the discarded e-waste was being loaded on pallets and then being loaded into a semi-trailer. A semi-trailer! Even with that, I still see residents leaving old monitors by the curbside on garbage day. With the proliferation of electronic gadgetry, shouldn't these types of events be held more often?

* Some electronic retailers have definitely made an effort to accept e-waste. But was it obvious when I visited one such store recently? Not really. There's a bin for old batteries. The slots would definitely not accommodate a scanner, printer or PC. The drop-off point is where?

* In the local grocery store, the organic and more earth-friendly selections are relegated to a special aisle. Yes, there's the point that by putting them there, it allows one to one-stop shop. Two problems here. First, the selections are scant. Second, this does not encourage the mainstream grocery buyer to consider a greener alternative. It per-

petuates the stereotype that being eco friendly makes one different.

What is obvious from all of these scenarios (and others that I'm sure you can add to the list) is that consumers are missing enough tools, resources, and opportunities to follow a greener lifestyle. What easy-to-go-green effort can you integrate into your business or community today—such as collection containers, rearrangement of offerings, or other convenience services—to help create greener consumers?

Being a role model by selecting more eco friendly promotions also goes a long way towards promoting green values to your colleagues and community.

CHAPTER 18: WHY CAN'T CONSUMERS IDENTIFY GREEN COMPANIES?

A disturbing article from a couple years ago reported on a survey that found a majority of consumers had a difficult time identifying "green" companies, in other words, companies that are known for their eco friendly initiatives. Not so surprising was that most of the companies consumers in the survey actually could name were those that provided groceries, household products, and automobiles. Two other key product categories, apparel and technology, were surprisingly absent from their minds.

So why is this?

I was not surprised at all that the scant few companies consumers could name. Watch television for any length of time and you'll see that some household cleaner will be advertised as being safe for your home or the environment. I would say that the ads for cleaning products are more prevalent than for food items. Plus, every car ad seems to tout the miles per gallon performance rating of their vehicle at the least. At the most, they're showing how earth friendly either the company or the car is.

I am also not surprised that apparel or technology companies were not easily identified either. From my experience in the promotional products arena, where apparel is a key segment of the industry, there are very few companies that are completely committed to greener products or manufacturing. The field has a myriad of smaller, lesser known organizations, or specialty market divisions within larger ones, that provide greener promotional wear... none of which are rolling off the tongues of the American public. The apparel industry is in dire need of re-inventing itself for both eco friendly and fair trade initiatives on every level, from supply chain to public relations. Good news is that lately I've been seeing more emphasis on USA manufactured wearable goods. At least it's a start.

Burning question for me is: How do consumers identify a "green" company or product in their minds? Is it a company that uses alternative energy or have a reputation for decreasing their carbon footprint? Are the products recyclable, biodegradable, non-toxic, or made from sustainable materials? Is the product made in a fair trade environment? Do consumers even really know was is meant by "green?"

I think companies in all markets are having a difficult time communicating their green-ness to the public. As well, I think many fear that if they don't get their green message right, they will be scolded for greenwashing.

Consumers will not learn about your earth and socially conscious efforts by ESP. Start telling them your green story!

CHAPTER 19:
HOW GREEN ARE PROMOTIONAL PRODUCTS NOW AND WHAT IS THEIR FUTURE?

Hard to believe that it's been over 40 years since the very first Earth Day in 1970. So where do I see the green movement, especially as it relates to promotional products and marketing?

Green Dollar Values Still Trump Green Values. I still see lots of people choosing green dollar values over green values. What's interesting is that even when times were better, people weren't hopping onto the green bandwagon in droves. Unless it's a huge deal for the company, such as if they are working on achieving a certain environmental standard, it's a nice to do, not a have to do, effort for promotional products. As well, prices are still higher for many more eco friendly products, although some are getting closer to their standard petroleum based cousins.

Small Efforts Are Gaining Some Ground. Maybe it's just choosing a reusable product over a disposable one. These small, easy to do efforts do seem to be gaining a foothold. Seeing lots more reusable bags at tradeshows and stores. In fact, in 2010 my company sold more reusable bags for events than ever.

Digital Marketing is Seen as a Panacea, But There's a Catch. Event and tradeshow people are flocking to digital marketing strategies such as those that use QR codes or mobile apps. But there's a big catch: You've got to get people to buy in. At a number of recent events I've done, I've included a big QR code in my booth. I can probably count on one hand the people who understood what it was or how to use it. Many times, I'd have to show them how to download a scanning app. And I really, really hate wasting my selling time showing someone how to use their own Blackberry or Android, sometimes iPhone, but rarely (not implying anything!). Often what I hear is *"I just bought this phone and I have no idea how to use it."* So I use these tools carefully, tailoring it to the anticipated audience.

Promotional USB Drives and Device Specific Promotions Will Continue to Lose Favor. On a related digital marketing note, promotional USB drives will continue to lose favor as mobile apps and more powerful smartphones saturate the market. And with devices getting updated constantly, focusing your promotion for use on a specific device could decrease the longevity and usefulness of your marketing, as well as waste your budget.

Green & Gross. While many people are willing to reuse containers, clothing, and more at home, they are not so willing to share or reuse personal items at events. This necessitates offering both recycled and new, as well as having to deal with cleaning and storing recycled items.

The Green Excuse for Not Marketing. This is hilarious. Sometimes when I'm soliciting promo business, I get the *"we're going green so we're not buying anything"* excuse. Yes, excuse. Please, people, admit you're running low on the other green (cash) and don't paint your non-activity as going green. Be authentic and take baby steps toward a greener marketing future!

ABOUT HEIDI THORNE

Hi! I'm Heidi Thorne, an author and business speaker. I have over 25 years of experience in sales, advertising, marketing and public relations, including a decade in the hospitality and trade show industries. As well, I sold promotional products for 17 years.

Books. I have written several books on business, geared for small business owners, entrepreneurs and consultants. For a current listing of all books, with links to purchasing, visit the "Books" page at HeidiThorne.com.

www.ingramcontent.com/pod-product-compliance
Lightning Source LLC
Chambersburg PA
CBHW051223170526
45166CB00005B/2023